FOOTPRINTS
IN THE SAND

A Journey to the Cross and Beyond

Words by Joseph M. Martin
Music by Joseph M. Martin & David Angerman
Orchestration Arranged by Brant Adams

CONTENTS

Performance Time: Approx. 45 minutes

GlorySound

EXCLUSIVELY DISTRIBUTED BY
HAL•LEONARD®
CORPORATION
7777 W. BLUEMOUND RD. P.O. BOX 13819 MILWAUKEE, WI 53213

Visit Shawnee Press Online at www.shawneepress.com

PERFORMANCE NOTES

"Footprints in the Sand" provides for the option of two narrators. One narrator presents Christ's journey through the reading of Scripture. The second narrator offers commentary connecting these scripture passages to the anthems themselves. You might choose to incorporate just one of these narrators depending on the desired performance duration and preferred narrative style. If both readers are used then it is recommended that two different vocal types be used to create contrast between the two readings.

If you wish to present the cantata during Holy Week you may want to consider ending the work with the anthem "Walk With Me." Following this anthem have one of the narrators or the pastor speak, "Jesus, You are the journey...and You are the journey's end. Amen." The final anthem "Pathway of Hope" anthem can then be presented on Easter to complete the work.

Please feel to adapt "Footprints in the Sand" in any way that would enhance the delivery of its message to your community of faith.

Joseph M. Martin

* NARRATOR 1:

"I am the Way, the Truth, and the Life." With this acclamation, Jesus established for all people the pathway of faith. These sacred words have become our pillar of light and truth through the wilderness of this world. His footprints in the sands of time are a golden trail that leads us into joy. Yes, Christ is the journey and He is the journey's end. Come let us walk together and we will follow the footsteps that lead to faith and beyond.

* In additon to or instead of being read, this narration may be printed in your bulletin. Your congregation might find it helpful to think on these words as they prepare for the presentation of "Footprints in the Sand."

Footprints in the Sand

Words by
JOSEPH M. MARTIN (BMI)

Music by
DAVID ANGERMAN (ASCAP)

Also available separately for S.A.T.B. voices: A6998

A8577

8

foot - prints in the sand___ that___ lead to Cal - va - ry.___ How

sand___

beau - ti - ful the feet___ Prince of

of the bless - ed Prince of Peace.___

Peace. I thank You, Lord,___ for Your foot - prints in the sand.___

Lord, as the new day dawns, I see You walk-ing by the crys-tal sea.

foot-prints in the sand___ by the sea of Gal - i - lee.___ There are

foot-prints in the sand___ that___ lead to Cal - va - ry!___ How

beau - ti - ful the feet___ of the bless-ed Prince of Peace.___

16

(This page was intentionally left blank.)

A8577

NARRATOR 1:

The people were waiting expectantly and wondering in their hearts if John might possibly be the Christ. John answered them all, "I baptize you with water, but One more powerful than I will come, whose sandals I am not worthy to untie."

When all the people were being baptized, Jesus was baptized too. And, as He was praying, heaven was opened and the Holy Spirit descended on Him in bodily form like a dove. And a voice came from heaven: "You are my Son, whom I love; with You I am well pleased."
Luke 3:15-17, 21-22

NARRATOR 2:

From the waters of baptism, the Savior emerged saturated with the Spirit of God. Drenched with purpose, He began His ministerial sojourn. With each perfect step, a pathway of hope was being established in the hearts of the people. Steadfastly, He moved onward into undiscovered territory, teaching the pilgrims who followed Him the way everlasting.

dedicated to the Glory of God and the observance of the 100th anniversary
of Grace United Church of Christ, Hanover, PA, July 9, 2006

The Master Has Come

Tune: THE ASH GROVE
Welsh Folk Tune
Arranged by
JOSEPH M. MARTIN (BMI)

Words by
SARAH DOUDNEY (1841-1926)

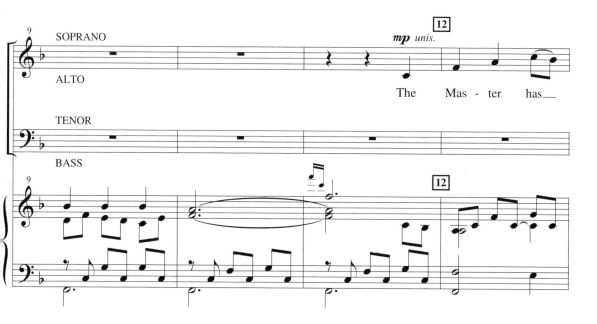

come, and He calls us to fol - low the track of the foot - prints He leaves on our way.

Far

o - ver the moun - tain and through the deep hol - low, the

path leads— us— on to the man - sions of day.

The— Mas - ter— has— called us the peo - ple— who—

trust Him, who march 'neath— Christ's ban - ner, His own lit - tle

band._____ We love Him, we__ seek Him, we

long to__ be__ near Him, and rest in__ the__ light of His

beau - ti - ful land.

God's Holy Spirit shall com-fort the wea-ry. We
fol-low the Sav-ior and can-not turn back. The
Mas-ter has called us. Though doubt and temp-ta-tion may
Come,* come, come, come. May

shall

com - pass__ our__ jour - ney, we cheer - ful - ly sing.__

"Press__ on - ward, look__ up - ward." Through much trib - u -

la - tion, the chil - dren__ of__ Zi - on must fol - low their

dew__ on the sod._____ We turn from the__

world,__ with__ its__ smiles__ and__ its__ scorn - ing,__ to cast in__ our__

cast__ our

lot__ with__ the__ peo - ple of God. The__

28

Mas - ter has__ called us His sons and__ His__ daugh - ters. We

plead for__ His__ bless - ing and trust in His love;__ _cresc._

with great celebration **ff** 117

___ and through the green__ pas - tures, be - side the__ still__

wa - ters,__ He'll__ lead us__ at__ last to His king - dom a -

bove._____ O the Mas - ter has

come!_____

126 *no rit. to end*

no rit. to end

NARRATOR 1:

Jesus returned to Galilee in the power of the Spirit, and news about Him spread through the whole countryside. He taught in their synagogues, and everyone praised Him.

The scroll of the prophet Isaiah was handed to Him, and He stood up to read. Unrolling it, He found the place where it is written: "The Spirit of the Lord is on Me because He has anointed Me to preach good news to the poor. He has sent Me to proclaim freedom for the prisoners and recovery of sight for the blind, to release the oppressed, to proclaim the year of the Lord's favor." *Luke 4:14-19*

NARRATOR 2:

The journey had begun. From town to town and village to village, Jesus went proclaiming the good news of the kingdom of God. As He went, He healed the sick and did many wonderful works. Traveling through the land, He gathered to Himself many followers from whom He chose twelve disciples. Together they began a sacred quest that would lead the world through the deserts of death and sin and into the glorious paradise of God's promised life. Everywhere He went, the people were amazed at His miracles and astonished at His teaching, for He spoke with great power.

for the dedication of the "Many Gifs, One Spirit" Facility Expansion,
St. Andrews United Church of Christ, Louisville, KY

Rise Up! Rejoice!

Words and music by
JOSEPH M. MARTIN (BMI)

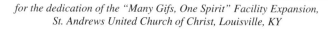

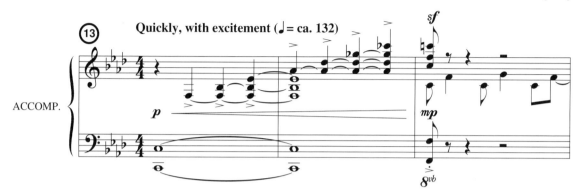

Rise up! Re-joice, ye chil - dren of Je - ho - vah!

Copyright © 2006, Malcolm Music
(a division of Shawnee Press, Inc., Nashville, TN)

Rise up! Re-joice, ye peo - ple of the Lamb.

Rise

Rise up! Re - joice and sing____ an al - le - lu - ia. Let the

up and sing____ an al - le - lu - ia. Let the

peo-ple pro-claim_ and re - joice in the name_ of the Lord!

34

man of peace and love?____ Be - hold the glo - ry

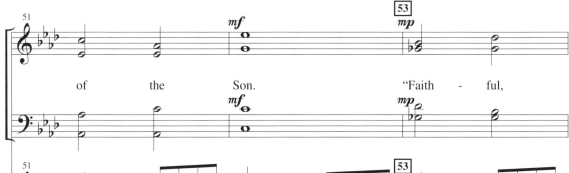

of the Son. "Faith - ful,

come. Seek - ers, come.

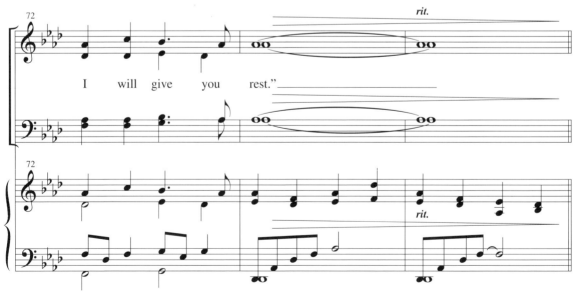

Come and let the cel - e - bra - tion start and nev - er end.

start,

Let the praise be - gin. Let the cel - e - bra - tion now be -

gin.

42

A8577

(This page was intentionally left blank.)

NARRATOR 1:

Then said Jesus to His disciples, "If anyone would come after Me, he must deny himself, take up his cross and follow Me. For whosoever will save his life shall lose it; and whosoever will lose his life for My sake shall find it." *Matthew 16:24*

NARRATOR 2:

Many followers began their journey with Jesus. Their first steps were confident and bold, but, as the path narrowed, it soon became evident that many parts of the road were filled with rocks and rough places. A number left the Way and abandoned the journey of faith. To those who remained, Jesus gave a vision of a road paved with tears. There were crosses waiting for all who would follow Him to the end. Yet through it all, they would never walk alone.

Songs for the Journey

Incorporating
"Guide Me, O Thou Great Jehovah"
"Savior, Like a Shepherd Lead Us"
and "He Leadeth Me"
Arranged by
JOSEPH M. MARTIN (BMI)

* Tune: BEACH SPRING, *The Sacred Harp*
Words: William Williams (1717-1791)

might - y; hold me with Thy pow'r-ful hand. Bread of

heav - en,___ Bread of heav - en,___ feed me till___ I want_ no

more.___ Bread of heav - en,___ Bread of heav - en, feed me

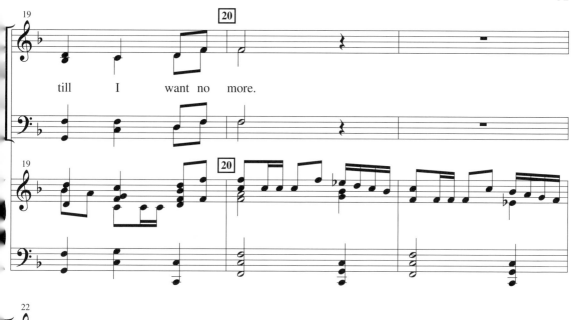

till I want no more.

Smoothly, with expression (♩ = ca. 80)

mp unis.

* Sav - ior, like a shep-herd

Smoothly, with expression (♩ = ca. 80)

* Tune: BRADBURY, William B. Bradbury (1816-1868)
  Words: Dorothy Thrupp (1779-1847)

lead____ us,____ much we need Thy ten-der care.

In Thy pleas-ant pas-tures feed____ us,____ for our use Thy folds pre-

pare. Bless-ed Je-sus! Bless-ed Je-sus! Thou hast

bought us, Thine we are._____ Bless-ed Je - sus! Bless-ed

Je - sus!_____ Thou hast bought us,

Thine we are.

54

* Tune: HE LEADETH ME, William Bradbury (1816-1868)
  Words: Joseph H. Gilmore (1834-1918)

A8577

I would be, for by His hand He lead - eth me.

ff 59 *with joyful abandon*

He lead - eth me, He lead - eth me, by

with joyful abandon

His own hand He lead - eth me. His

faith - ful __ fol - l'wer I would __ be, for by His __ hand __ He __

lead - eth _____ me. He lead-eth me.

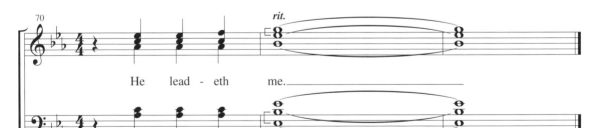

He lead - eth me. _____

(This page was intentionally left blank.)

NARRATOR 1:

And when they drew nigh unto Jerusalem, a very great multitude spread their garments in the way; others cut down branches from trees and placed them on the road. And the multitudes that went before, and that followed, cried, "Hosanna to the Son of David: Blessed is He who comes in the name of the Lord." *Matthew 21:1-9*

NARRATOR 2:

As the road approached the great holy city, Jesus was met by a vast parade of people shouting and praising God. The triumphant arrival of the promised King excited the whole city. As one great procession, they moved toward the temple, and, for a moment, it appeared that Christ's final destination would be the palace of an earthly kingdom. Unwavering, the Savior walked past the marbled halls to His divine destiny. Soon the road would begin its twisted trek into a valley deep with shadows.

commissioned for the 150th Anniversary of First United Methodist Church,
New Braunfels, Texas, which was founded in 1853 by German immigrants

Lift High Your Songs of Praise

Tune: VRUECHTEN
David's Psalmen, 1685
Arranged by
DAVID ANGERMAN (ASCAP)
and JOSEPH M. MARTIN (BMI)

Words by
JOSEPH M. MARTIN

Also available for S.A.T.B. voices: A7682

A8577

Sing— a— glad ho-san-na! Lift

high your songs of praise!___ Let all the peo-ple— crown the King with

glo- ry! Lift up your heads, ye gates,___ you

ev - er - last - ing__ doors de - clare the__ sto - ry!

Wave palms of praise on high. Lay down your hearts be - fore the

Lord! Let glad ho - san - nas ring for Je - sus Christ is

mp *cresc. poco a poco*

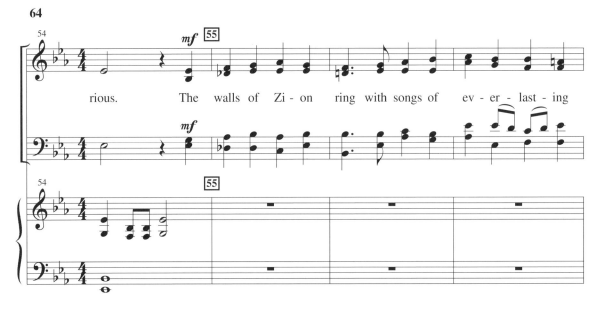

NARRATOR 1:

It was just before the Passover Feast. Jesus knew that the time had come for Him to leave this world and go to the Father. Having loved His own who were in the world, He now showed them the full extent of His love.

As the evening meal was being served, He got up from the table, took off His outer clothing, and wrapped a towel around His waist. After that, He poured water into a basin and began to wash His disciples' feet, drying them with the towel that was wrapped around Him. "Do you understand what I have done for you?" He asked them. "You call Me 'Teacher' and 'Lord,' and rightly so, for that is what I am. Now that I, your Lord and Teacher, have washed your feet, you also should wash one another's feet. I have set you an example that you should do as I have done for you." *John 13:1-15*

NARRATOR 2:

In the flickering candlelight of an upper room, the journey-weary pilgrims at last rested. Taking on the role of servant, The Creator knelt before His creation. With the tears of grace He gently washed the disciples' feet. The dust of the journey fell away and, refreshed by the cleansing waters and the Savior's healing touch, the disciples were ready to rest at the table of grace.

Come to the Table of Grace

Music by
JOSEPH M. MARTIN (BMI)
DAVID ANGERMAN (ASCAP)
and DOUGLAS NOLAN (BMI)

Words by
JOSEPH M. MARTIN
and DOUGLAS NOLAN

Also available for S.A.T.B. voices: A7943

A8577

68

A8577

70

A8577

Grace, grace is a ban - quet, and Je - sus came to share!

All who are bro - ken, who

72

A8577

Come to the ta-ble of grace.

One in the Spir-it and one in His love, come to the ta-ble of

ban - quet, and Je - sus came____ to share.

All who are hun-gry, who long to be fed,

NARRATOR 1:

And when they came to a place named Gethsemane, Jesus said to His disciples, "My soul is exceeding sorrowful unto death. Tarry here, watch while I go ahead and pray." And He went forward a little and fell on the ground and prayed that, if it were possible, the hour might pass from Him. *Mark 14:32-35*

NARRATOR 2:

As Jesus walked through the garden of shadows, did He remember that long ago Eden where He walked in the cool of the day seeking His creation? As He gazed at the thorny bushes that surrounded Him, did He consider the piercing price of sin, the sting of death and the deep sadness of a paradise lost? As He struggled with His Father's will, did He have a glimpse of the lonesome road that was stretching out before Him; a solitary way, that led to a rugged tree and another garden path…a desolate, jagged road that ended abruptly at the darkened entrance of a stone cold tomb?

The Garden Path

Words and music by
JOSEPH M. MARTIN (BMI)

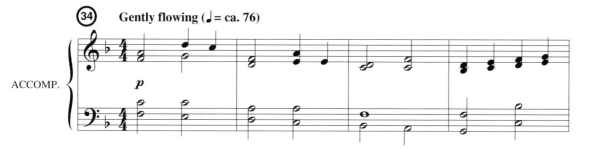

Copyright © 2006, Malcolm Music
(a division of Shawnee Press, Inc., Nashville, TN)

A8577

Sav - ior walked a - lone, pray - ing to His Fa - ther,___

"Let Thy will be done."

Sur - round - ed by the night, He

knelt in ag - o - ny, know - ing that the way of grace would

84

A8577

NARRATOR 1:

And as they led Him away, they laid hold on one whose name was Simon and on him they laid His cross, that he might bear it after Jesus… and when they had come to the place which is called Golgotha…there they crucified Him. *Matthew 27: 32-33*

NARRATOR 2:

It was called the way of sorrows. On this winding cruel course, Jesus fell from the weight of the cross and from the burden of sin that He had taken upon His heart. As His followers watched from afar, He gave Himself freely for the sins of the world. It was there upon that windswept hill that grace at last completed its journey.

Come Walk With Me

Tune: O WALY WALY
Traditional English Melody
Arranged by
JOSEPH M. MARTIN (BMI)

Words by
JOSEPH M. MARTIN

trails_____ of Gal - i - lee, where Je - sus

walked_____ His__ earth - ly days. Come walk with

(end solo)

me. Come walk with me.

Come walk with me _____ down paths of stone. Come climb the

hill _____ of Cal - va - ry.

There Je - sus

bore _____ His cross a - lone. Come walk with

(This page was intentionally left blank.)

NARRATOR 1:

On the third day, two of the disciples went traveling to a village called Emmaus. It came to pass that, while they walked, Jesus Himself drew near and went with them. Unrecognized by them, He began to expound upon all the scriptures and the things concerning Himself. Suddenly, their eyes were opened and they knew Him. And, arising the same hour, they returned to Jerusalem, found the other disciples and those who were gathered with them saying, "the Lord is risen indeed!"

NARRATOR 2:

Therefore be followers of Christ as dear children, holding to His grace-scarred hands and clinging to His love as you go along life's way. May hope be your constant companion and may you always walk in the light as He is in the light until you come to His promised rest. Jesus, You are the journey…and You are the journey's end. Amen!

written for the Sanctuary Choir and Orchestra of Sunny Lane United Methodist Church,
Del City, Oklahoma in celebration of their church's 50th Anniversary, Chris Moore, Director

Pathway of Hope

Words and music by
JOSEPH M. MARTIN (BMI)

Also available for S.A.T.B. voices: A7474

Copyright © 2000, 2006, Malcolm Music
(a division of Shawnee Press, Inc., Nashville, TN)

You are the jour-ney. Come walk be-side us as we go._____ Lord, You are the way. You are the jour-ney. You are our leg-a-cy,

We'll walk the road as one._____ And when we've walked ten thou - sand years, the jour - ney will have just be - gun._____